My Mojave

MY MOJAVE

POEMS BY
Donald Revell

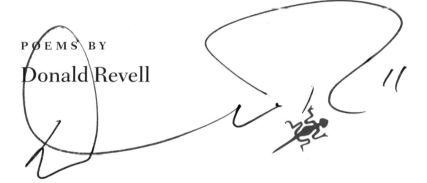

Alice James Books

FARMINGTON, MAINE

ACKNOWLEDGMENTS
The author thanks the editors of the following journals in whose pages many of these poems first appeared:

American Letters & Commentary: "The Arts of Peace" and "31.xii.99"; *American Poetry Review*: "Pandemonium," "Prolegomena," "The Kingdom," "Sermon," "Ayre," and "Meadowork"; *Antioch Review*: "My Trip"; *Barrow Street*: "Heat like Murder" and "Mechanics"; *Black Warrior Review*: "Arcady Again," "Just Leaving," *"Timor Mortis Conturbat Me,"* "Matins," "Counsel," "To the Destroyers of Ballots," "In Christmas 2000," and "A New Abelard"; *Conduit*: "Harvest"; *Conjunctions*: "For Thomas Traherne" and "For Andrew Marvell"; *Fence*: "The Government of Heaven"; *Greensboro Review*: "Church and State"; *Harvard Review*: "Picnic"; *Luna*: "Pause Going North" and "Bacchae"; *Volt*: "Banner" and "Short Fantasia"; *Washington Square*: "Moving Day"

"Timor Mortis Conturbat Me" was also published as a broadside by Sutton Hoo Press.

10 9 8 7 6 5 4 3 2 1

Alice James Books are published by Alice James Poetry Cooperative, Inc., an affiliate of the University of Maine at Farmington.

ALICE JAMES BOOKS
238 MAIN STREET
FARMINGTON, MAINE 04938

www.alicejamesbooks.org

Alice James Books gratefully acknowledges support from the University of Maine at Farmington and the National Endowment for the Arts.

LIBRARY OF CONGRESS CATALOGING-IN-PUBLICATION DATA
Revell, Donald, 1954–
My Mojave : poems / by Donald Revell.
    p.   cm.
ISBN 1–882295–40–4
I. Title.
PS3568.E793 M9 2003
811'.54—dc21   2002015864

COVER IMAGE: Fairfield Porter (American, 1907–1975), Primroses, © 1963–64. Oil on canvas, 30 x 24 in. The Parrish Art Museum, Southampton, N.Y., Gift of the Estate of Fairfield Porter, 1980.10.85. Photo credit: Jim Strong, Inc.

to Claudia,

and in memory of her father,

Edward Thomas Keelan, Jr.

CONTENTS

Arcady Again

Beside the house a path
Green leaves as low
As my eyes and a low
Gate into the rainy yard
Opens and even the little
Grass is very wide

God help the man who breathes
With nothing leading him
Here or someplace like it
Inside him which he opens
Wide enough to walk through
And walks through

Surprised to find deer and turtles
Living so near his house

HERE

Heaven might be defined as the place which men avoid.

—Henry David Thoreau

Pandemonium

Some natural tears they dropped,
Especially on the 900 block of Fairchild
Where a bicycle leans against a broken Aphrodite
On porch-steps.

Behind them it was a jumble
Coming into flower and brown fences
Breaking like waves at all angles
And rooftops at all angles.

A sustained applause, and heartfelt,
Began only when they had gone.

2.

A fond study of the public swingsets
Lags behind wild grasses
Growing to change them to pleasures
Of depths of fire.

I remember my son in tears
In the apple tree, ashamed
Because he could not climb it,
Not realizing he had already climbed it

And was being photographed in the blossoms
Eight feet above violets and dandelions.

3.

There was a postman told me
How to find mushrooms good for pickling
On the days after heavy rains
Wherever elms lay fallen.

There was another man, Reverend Fate,
Interim pastor of Main Street Congregational.
That's all I know about him, but his sermons
Are shirts for my pillow, my dream sermons.

If I unleaf what he has spoken,
It is all about constancy.

4.

The first disobedience is always best,
A kind of providence, okay,
And a lampshade upside down
On a polished table. Afterwards,

Everything is shiny poor repairs.
Steps and letterboxes. Steps half in shade
And half in bright sunlight, wandering
Very deliberately but wandering

Among fallen trees and boys climbing.
Taking their leave, the parents join hands in a picture taken.

Mechanics

What neighborhood? Only death and trees, or one
Tree. Someone explained to me the difference
East from West is the imagination
Of a single tree as against a forest.
Was he smiling? The Californians settle
Like a gold ash upon their pine woods.
A stone's throw west of Melville's tomb, my father's
Headstone tilts under one spruce kept alive
By sprinklerheads and a Puerto Rican gardener.
The gardener sings in the accent of his ocean.
At Big Sur, there are too many sounds to count one.
The forest is countless. A tree is almost none.
This is the house that Jack built East to West.
He was smiling, and his teeth were planted in rows.

My Trip

I am looking at a smallpox vaccination scar
In a war movie on the arm
Of a young actor. He has just swum
Across a river somewhere in Normandy
Into the waiting arms of his rejoicing comrades.

Of course, the river's in California,
And the actor is dead now. Nevertheless,
This is the first of many hotels this trip,
And I find myself preferring wars
To smut on the networks,
Even as I find myself reading
The Pisan Cantos for the umpteenth time
Instead of the novel in my bag.
The poet helps me to the question:
Does anything remain of home at home?

Next day is no way of knowing,
And the day after is my favorite,
A small museum really perfect
And a good meal in the middle of it.
As I'm leaving,
I notice a donkey on a vase
Biting the arm of a young girl,
And outside on the steps
A silver fish head glistens beside a bottlecap.
Plenty remains.

The work of poetry is trust,
And under the aegis of trust
Nothing could be more effortless.
Hotels show movies.
Walking around even tired
I find my eyes find
Numberless good things
And my ears hear plenty of words
Offered for nothing over the traffic noise
As sharp as sparrows.

A day and a day, more rivers crossing me.
It really feels that way, I mean
I have changed places with geography,

And rivers and towns pass over me,
Showing their scars, finding their friends.
I like it best when poetry
Gleams or shows its teeth to a girl
Forever at just the right moment.
I think I could turn and live underneath the animals.
I could be a bottlecap.

Going to the airport going home,
I stop with my teacher, now my friend.
He gives me a good breakfast, berries and hotcakes.
We finish and, standing, I hear
One policeman saying to another
Over the newspaper in a yellow booth
"Do you know this word *regret*, Eddie?
What does it mean?"
Plenty of words over the traffic noise,
And nothing could be more effortless.
Catching a glimpse of eternity, even a poor one, says it all.

31.xii.99

Satisfaction glories aloft and my ground
Is brittle winter verbena
Whoever walks on it purges himself
To enter the temples anywhere

In Las Vegas pictures arrive from Moscow
St Basil's crazy affiliations
Glow in the fireworks and small snow

Aloft at midnight midnight moves
Across the planet seeking monuments
And an unmistaken early-flowering tree

Some verbena catches fire from rockets
An uncomprehending New Year's baby gestures
Urging God to be God-like
Earth to be worthy a grown man's living there

The Kingdom

An early day moved me
To Blue River
A good place now
They've given the waterhouse
Away to the Falls, and grass
Is for any horse that wants it.

The Falls winked out.
I was kicked.
Killed for a time, I studied with nobody.
I gave a house away.
You say you are not a Lincoln man, but still would like
To have Mr. Lincoln's autograph. Well, here it is.

Finding by accident a lady
Sleeping on horseback, her expression
Foretelling your future character
(People have characters just as rivers
Falls), remember Lincoln and his burdens.
Kingdoms move inside men.

Moving Day

My bed abandoned
On a ranch road
Waits for anyone,
And they should hurry.
It's a good bed.
If the roads were level
I'd have it still.

Not half so lucky,
The teapot's in pieces
In a trash barrel.
It was *white* white
When I bought it
And I was new to poetry
Twenty years ago.

We're not home yet.
And I'm still new
To my callings:
Teacher, drunkard, absent minister.
I was in Carcassonne once.
I saw two horses there
And God who invented them.

My Mojave

Sha-
Dow,
As of
A meteor
At mid-
Day: it goes
From there.

A perfect circle falls
Onto white imperfections.
(Consider the black road,
How it seems white the entire
Length of a sunshine day.)

Or I could say
Shadows and mirage
Compensate the world,
Completing its changes
With no change.

In the morning after a storm,
We used brooms. Out front,
There was broken glass to collect.
In the backyard, the sand
Was covered with transparent wings.
The insects could not use them in the wind
And so abandoned them. Why
Hadn't the wings scattered? Why
Did they lie so stilly where they'd dropped?
It can only be the wind passed through them.

Jealous lover,
Your desire
Passes the same way.

And jealous earth,
There is a shadow you cannot keep
To yourself alone.
At midday,
My soul wants only to go
The black road which is the white road.
I'm not needed
Like wings in a storm,
And God is the storm.

Church and State

Where boys throw stones today
And a sparkle rises to each stone
The river is among itself
Like some creature
With a pure empty power
To sleep sometimes even
As it moves or as it hunts.

Town is really near
Across the road. The motel
Where yesterday two children
Burned to death is closed with barricades,
And the church next door is covered with ribbons.
From porches and lampposts
Flags mark the Fourth of July which is today.

Almost everybody in town
Answers the church bell.
After a while the boys
Come up from the river
Hauling a tire into the sunlight.
Because of the heat
The church windows are open top and bottom.
A beautiful sound
Comes outside. It's no effort
To sing the hymns ourselves, and we do that.

Short Fantasia

The plane descending from an empty sky
Onto numberless real stars
Makes a change in heaven, a new
Pattern for the ply of spirits on bodies.
We are here. Sounds press our bones down.
Someone standing recognizes someone else.
We have no insides. All the books
Are written on the steel beams of bridges.
Seeing the stars at my feet, I tie my shoes
With a brown leaf. I stand, and I read again
The story of Aeneas escaping the fires
And his wife's ghost. We shall meet again
At a tree outside the city. We shall make
New sounds and leave our throats in that place.

Just Leaving

At sunrise the high branches of the trees
Fill with sparkles, and wide seagulls screech
Hundreds of miles from any ocean.
The city breaks the street we climbed the night
Our son came. Late this afternoon, he and I
Will play there, covering ourselves with dust.
As I do every day and more than once,
I think of *The Iliad*. Terrible
In all ways, it remains a morning book
Open to the unused violence
Of early things. But later today, when Ben
Throws dust into my hair, I will look
To see Priam old and Achilles
Old equally, his killing done, his limbs loose.

Meadowork

American flowers pallid in a cloud
Showed pink until the shadows moved
And it was red morning, colored
After Christ's own heart.

        Beneath the shadows, something traveling,
        In the near distance, someone kissing a doorpost
        Cried aloud

PITYS
A girl's name.
Pan loved her
Because she walked like butterflies,
Shaking herself in the pines

        Beneath the shadows,
        In the near distance,
        Loud.

The trees were coming into shape, all shadow.
I was telling my son
A dead flower isn't the corpse of a flower

        Because long ago
        A bad king locked a shepherd
        In a cedarwood chest,
        And the bees flew
        In from the fields
        And fed the shepherd
        Flowers through the cracks.

Son, a dead flower isn't the corpse of a flower,
And at the end of the day, dusk
Will come like smoke around
And still not put out the roses.

The Government of Heaven

"the grass is higher than here"
—WILLIAM CARLOS WILLIAMS

I.

One and soon
Another hummingbird
Alights very near

They do not stir
In the branches anymore
For a long time

This is really the world
In June 2000
Ours and mine

Needing all the same
The government of Heaven
So many other trees
Are filled with obscenities
Disappointed things
Naked as the bodies
I sometimes see instead
Of men and women

Something governs the hummingbird so well
She delights in stillness
Even moving she barely moves

Something fades my son's wet fingermark
From the warm stone

And then more obscenities

2.

Promises concealed
Are skin (this from Sir Walter Raleigh)
So full of rivers it carries sugar

Let Greeks be Greeks
And women what they are
Fences thrill at the view

I make no argument
I ache only for silence just one
With nothing to forgive

For years I have pictured it by a river
Secret to America and wholly American
A shore of pines and one of birches
Sunlight very fast and white in between

The people are like berries and no handmarks
They are carnations
The river bathes them white as sugar
And no handmarks
Breasts bow to where the water sparkles
Governor my heart stops

River of mandate
Golden Age
But sunshine doesn't warm the stones
And there are no birds

3.

Completing the scene
Is a tree surrounded
By bones of horses
Slaughtered like sacrifices
Even these are white and clean
Beside the obscenities
Summer of 2000
Heat sharper than winter cold
Heat like murder

America seems an undersea without rivers

Kingfisher's secret name is Jack Iago

And as Charles Darwin good man
Born the very same day as Abraham Lincoln
Wrote "three species of tyrant-flycatchers
(Are) a form strictly American"

The fleshy sweetness comes and not a memory it really comes to me
As you might come to a booth in a swamp
Then a river might appear
And then the whole business of appearance would destroy
    politics
Giving absolute sovereignty to the love of God
For wild horses Greeks women and fences

Governor your handiwork stops and starts my heart
In the secret intervals may this country really move

4.

October 1, 2000 walking the dog
In deep shade I see 100 yds ahead
In bright sunlight a red clown hitchhiking
But of course it's a fireplug
I could never say the word
"Clown" I said "Keenoo"
Pointing at the circus parade
On the pediatrician's wallpaper
(Rest in peace Robert Lax
Circus poet died this past week)
The dog and I were startled then
By the chiding of a big crow
In the branches overhead
And we started walking again

The French have especially loved American Negroes
Mine is a French family
Caw
How I love you
How the government of Heaven
Rests this morning in a crow's mouth

And in truth there can be no greater reward
For doing well than to be enabled to do well

Actual photograph of entertainer

5.

Waters overplussed with pilgrim stutter
Make more wilderness
The wood outside and oceans in

My saintly Billy
They hung my saintly Billy

In the Las Vegas phonebooks whores
Listed as "entertainers" show
Their faces sometimes
"Actual photograph of entertainer"
My mind stutters obscenities with names naked as bodies

The plot is the stutter
Is why
The wild is why

As a child I was afraid of the mantis
Not afraid that it might hurt me but instead
I might by accident destroy one
The mantis was protected by laws
And police cars cruised our streets

Saintly Billy
(We could not watch the movie of *Billy Budd* death so inevitable
    in all the actual faces)

We are corrupt as Europe
Eating one another as they do there—Thos. Jefferson

6.

Lord dear Governor God
The elections come very near now
And still in the heavy leaf fall
And on all the pretty young people
Walking avenues of the deep color
I conjure more precise obscenities
Cruelties really sad as all liberty
Is sad without worship

On March 7, 1835 at least Charles Darwin
Discovered the afterlife of Billy Budd
"It was the most laughable thing I ever heard. If the ship's crew
    had been all captains, and no men,
there could not have been a greater uproar of orders. We
    afterwards found that the mate stuttered. I
suppose all hands were assisting him in giving his orders."

October 20, 2000 Iowa City
I go out and I feel that every step of mine
Spoils the rime across the grass

In the government of Heaven
The grass is truly higher than here
Stones are warm as a circus
The kingfisher's common name is Abraham Lincoln
My son leaves a mark on everything
A shore of pines and one of birches
Where my rough feet shall Thy smooth praises sing

To the Destroyers of Ballots

For his cancer
My dog drinks
A wild tea
Of fallen leaves
In standing water

But this morning
We found ice
And underneath it
Nothing to drink
Only brittle leaves

No birds today
Except hawks keeping
A brown watch
Over no prey
Man and dog

Picnic

The story of my life is untrue but not
Thanksgiving Day when the bee fell in the bottle.
All days take instruction from accident.
My wife opened the red wine in a good spot
We found as we were hiking along a dry
Creekbed. She filled our cups as I cut
Bread and apples. We saw the bee dive
Into the green bottleneck and start
To swim. Then we spoke about children and ways to move
An old piano north to where our nephews live.
We finished the wine, and the bee was still alive.
I tapped him onto the ground, and he walked off
Untangling antennae from wings and wine.
We hurried to reach the car while there was still daylight.

Timor Mortis Conturbat Me

Tropical licorice

Inside me

Two places

Only one

With thee

Sweet

Rotted bougainvillea

Good outside

THERE

The knife which slices the bread of Jove ceases to be a knife when this service is rendered.

—Henry David Thoreau

Sermon

20,000 feet above them
I remember them really
Cooing like birds in their small shirts
And their mother on the bus
Laughing loving them
Her own shirt no bigger than theirs

We must make ways
Passengers and paracletes
To land the airplanes
Between human souls and children
To rain down still alive
The sexual memory which invented

Transport and places each of us
Into shirts too small and wingspans
Impossible for human bodies
Laughing out of mothers' mouths
Making their way from childhood
Into 20,000 feet and more of sky

Nothing to do with pity
Everything to do with heaven
An instance of motion not moved
But given by mouth and all the other skins
At risk at the mercy of operators
The way that logs love fires

For Thomas Traherne

The ground is tender with cold rain
Far and equally
Our coastlines grow younger
With tides
Beautiful winter
Not becoming spring today and not tomorrow
Has time to stay

Easter will be very late this year
Thirty years ago
I saw my church
All flowery
And snow
Melting in the hair of the procession
As tender as today

A sight above all festivals or praise
Is earth everywhere
And all things here
Becoming younger
Facing change
In the dark weather now like winter
Candling underground as rain

For Andrew Marvell

Lustrous tiger of swordplay is just a stick
On a sandpile
I remember because everything is all of its characteristics
Apart just once
Together for eternity in death's unlimited magic

Ilex conjures acanthus
I've never tasted quince I like the Snow Apple
Filled with sirocco
An austere example

And my son knows
In his tigerish swordplay
Once apart as I board the usual airplane
I remember
Magic I've taken from his hand and pressed like sharp sharp sand
    into mine

Banner

I turned a poor moth
Out of the window
Into a shower of rain
To save it from the candles

Say now aftermath
And a new beginning
One and the same
Happy like a crocus

I can be precise
Though it is no answer
Wreckage and young flowers
Fire and rain as the song goes

Like sliding in winter
Onto an iced meadow
With all that slipping
And happy tossing at the bottom

I can be precise
But aftermath and beginnings
Escape in the sparkles
Making no answer

What a banner for me
Blows
On a moth's wing
Leading me

Prolegomena

Always the last figurine,
Almost an afterthought,
The youngest shepherd
Is set down by the youngest child
At the edge of the nativity.
Far from the manger and well
Outside the yellowy circle
Of incandescent angels,
He looks away, watching,
It seems, for the stray mother
Of a dozy lamb on his shoulders.
Here, I would learn,
And not on the crucifix
Or on a glory of clouds,
Is the first image of the God-man
Jesus to come down to us.
In some museum or other,
The rough statuette of a boy
Continues now as then beginning
Centuries of worship and worry.
Virgil knew. And Virgil got it
From Theocritus as I got it
From figurines below a lighted tree.
And the earliest congregations knew it
Without asking. Giving thanks
Is later than a prayer.
And prayer is not yet.

2.

I had a dream the laws had legs
And arms and they were carrying pigs.
It looked like vengeance to me,
Out of touch with the tender confusions
And lamb-likeness of reality.

I speak to my poem now.
Tell me your dream.

Adjectival, cultless,
Ill-defined and filled
With animals, it marks
Me off. Before I was human,
I worshipped everything.
I knew the difference
Between two and three.
And one was a woman.

I tell my poem
Three are heavy
And do not dance well.

Poem says
A white umbrella
Is a slim foundation for festivals.

And any way you look at it, you are,
Like a heron on one leg, halfway to Jehovah.

3.

The beauties of the world advertise its poisons:
This dozen of strawberries,
These two letters remaining
Of a Greek inscription
Never to be deciphered.

We are among heroes,
But who they are
It is impossible to say
Until the poison works.

We came to a natural bridge and the air was instantly twenty
    degrees cooler. We walked on, and the
walls of the valley began to sweat and to wear red flowers. The
    place became too beautiful to leave,
and so we made an offering.

What can the inscription have described?
Telling is selling,
Even just two letters,
Very different from two birds
Hunting over the valley.

We made an offering, and a snake came out of its hole, and the
    birds killed it. As for describing it . . .

The beauties are falling away
In the shape of a heart unequally divided,
Animals to one side,
The Lord God Almighty on the other,
And me sitting in Missouri reading Dorothy not Wm Wordsworth.

4.

The little things of the woodland live unseen
At my soul's edge because the soul is alone
In the grass and loveliness, unwinding
Itself in their eyes where the edge moves.
I want to go to the invisible and see it.
In Greece, every dead hero was a snake.
They suffered their inspiration, and then Bromios,
God of sounds and voices, found them names.
Who am I to be seen without shouting?
What use is knowledge disappearing down a hole?
Come out and be killed, poem says.
You'll find company. Three ash trees
I saw beside a lake in late October.
One was bare. One was flame-red. The third
Smoldered still in summer green, and it was screaming.

5.

Imagination is the agony of meaning.
One by one, the lynxes are weeded out.
At sunrise, a white boy climbs
A heap of carcasses and sings.
Women climb and kill him.

Poem says
A sudden sheen in the delectable mts
Means the birds are awake.
It's settled.

But I get tired all the same,
Just as the women got tired
Of plagues and became the Muses.
I think all the time of a man,
Dylan Thomas, tangled in the sharp branches
Of a photograph, unable to bear
The memory of Heaven a moment longer.

Compared to Heaven,
Music and peace are shit.
Sheep graze on magic.
Birds shine a light.
I mean to choose
Between a famine and a poison sunshine.
O good shepherd,
Magic me.

6.

Always the last to arrive,
The Orpheus, the hillside ploughman,
Shepherds me too.
Poem says
He will be the death of me.
Heaven's heron starves, and while it starves
It glows.

Here's company.
They come to the stable; it is almost time.
For a last few moments, God is a wild thing
Or still a flower.
And then arrives a beautiful boy.
I see his wagon
Now in this now in that animal.

Counsel

Redress my soul
As in a mirror
I can see myself
Urging a friend
To stay alive

Just a few days
My new Buddha
Floats in marigolds
Until the August heat
Kills them

Remember friend
True grief is endless
As happiness
Is unforgettable
Every single time

Pause Going North

Beautiful lake without dimension only cloud

And jagged shore intervening so early

It is all one motion i.e. nothing moving

Every element outlined by Heaven

With the sun rising in every direction

Upon boats and 100,000 birds

The void is filled in less than a moment

Matins

Like magnets
Morning purposes
Are plain
Chains of metal
Rings or pieces
Of clothing
Fluttering
On a briar
No defeat
No abandoning
Our dead
Only plain purposes
And animals
One philosopher
Lucretius going crazy
In the hedgerow
Thinking of animals
Used in war

Bacchae

Earth make no mts more
But fires
And the grasses
To feed them.

Have you seen
The red grass
After an earthquake
Craze the wind?

O my soul
We are too deep in
The delectable mts
To see what comes.

Harvest

The god grows with us preparing
Answers to questions none will ask
Or only the winged beetle
In desert summer air
Too warm for anyone to breathe

Aversion then compulsion then
Children exchange childish blood
For coronets grown with God
It is cool enough to breathe now
It is autumn for the taking

In Christmas

1.

They were miserable comforters
Cardinals the only birds remaining
In bare trees and abandoned nests
Exposed to everything
Their brightness often a stab
Of the grotesque
More than sweet persistence
I should have seen.

And I saw the mountains burning up and the rubbish
And the people trampling over their own food
In front yards and in parks and in school yards.
How is Christ to come
To fumes
And cold prayers
All fires wasted on harms and obscurities
The American famine?

2.

Heavenly man
I am scarce to go
And well to stand
In a disused place.

Miserable cardinals comfort
The broken seesaws
And me who wants no comfort
Only to believe.

3.

The stream is frozen because it is cold.
The leaves are black and tufted like sea-waves
Because of wind and ice.
Heavenly man
The toys of the disused places
The seesaws and cowardly birds
Afraid to fly from winters and fires
Welcome you.

You will famish us from words
And from crooks and underbarrows
And from owls and dragons at night
And from the horses snuffing up
Fat and full with judgement.
Send all away
Until your friends are alone with their famine
Every day because of today.

Ayre

The robin combines two hymns
At the cross
Dead gone on me
Rich as Croesus
Ponder these

Joseph's coat
Apostle
Mater
Work fast
Speed along

The other cheek spat on her
O glory of the snow
Go with Mary
Letters of the law
Go with Mary

A New Abelard

1.

God watch
I am in the basement of fog
And shall act
Between enthusiasm and dismay
I call attention
To your pile of hoard
The really beautiful
Like the Egyptian poem
This morning coming true
And you know I am not looking

2.

God eat our suffering
Out of which we churn butter
See
How troubles twin us
The white doe
Afraid
The National Bank
Afraid
Although the soul we have
Is love's doing

3.

Start right now
If you are a twig
Start now
Protest
Skins and skins of death
Offer you
Our life it is what we fight for
With sun
The only stain in it
Taking out pain which was not accurate

4.

This is porcelain ground
Walk on it
You are more steep
Now than we were
Struggle I suppose
However close
Your vision and ours
Handsome one
This ground is the continuing struggle
Loving it

5.

Season
Cello
Shield
Trio
Somewhere
There is alive
At this moment
Some new St Francis
Law of object of a leaf
If he is unleafed

6.

A man walking over snow
Makes his way painfully
To a wooden shed
The door nearly
Comes off in his hand
When he grasps the handle
Inside
Rotten machinery sparkles with the damp
The iron smell is warm
To Almighty God it is Christmas afternoon

7.

Twig white
Doe trio
With sun the only stain in it
We are a protest
Raised against ourselves
And God comes now
And God is alone in a leaf
And we are snow in the desert
Making a new sound

Heat like Murder
(from the Journals of Dorothy Wordsworth)

The sun shone

                                                 unfit

for it   I thought I would get

the visit over

                                   and I went

off. I had a very pleasant walk—

                  The wind

      was covered all over   bright silver waves

                                 then

others rose up and took their place

              The Rocks

                  must be a holy place, etc. etc.

I had many very exquisite feelings   I saw

lofty hills, with that bright   light

and tried to write

The Arts of Peace

Engraving of a bull's head
Is surrounded
By a water stain
Shaped exactly
Like a lion's head.

This on the cover
Of a library book
Virgil's *Georgics*
1940 translation
Made in Great Britain.

Draw your own conclusions.
Water does.
Sometimes books
Are true because of rain.

Given Days

The attacks were tall, and then they burned.
I'd been reading, and then it was time
To take my son to school before the mustangs,
As they do every day, fled
The schoolyard for quieter fields up high.

The news was far, then close.
Something had towered above the sky,
And now the sky was alone. At bedtime,
I began to read where I'd broken off:
Walt Whitman, a kosmos, of Manhattan the son . . .

Somewhere between, a little before dinner,
I'd gone out walking.

I passed the fat lady and her lovely daughter,
A three-year old, on the stoop where they spend every day.
Between them was an orange with a face cut into it,
A tiny jack-o-lantern five weeks early.

A kosmos

Suspended in 1912, the Brooklyn Ferry resumes tomorrow,
And the sky reclaims its own,
And the river reclaims its own,
And we are the despised.

Strange new flight paths

        chains of the smallest pearls

And glint of the Colorado

        small so
      chained so

YOU COULD IMAGINE A CHILD'S DOWNY WRIST

Where never before
Mist showed over water
To the east of our wings

YOU COULD SEE THE CHILD
(Village of Blue Diamond, Nevada)
RUNNING WITH MUSTANGS

Signs of the times, no, these are brighter, these are heavens and
    damn all murderers.

October 22, 2001

I am angry (10/22

        The house I was raised in
        Still my mother's alone house
        1022 Vincent Avenue, Bronx, New York

With my dog for being angry
At Jack Spicer on the radio
Or afraid

Under the table with his diarrhea
And his bandanna covered with jack-o-lanterns

> *The house is falling away*
> *My father's death my sister's death the*
> *Halloween I was ill*
> *And doled out treats in my devil's suit to the*
> *healthy children*
> *And our turtle died under a Woolworth*
> *palm tree in a Woolworth pond*

"Believe the birds"
All's well now the dog's asleep now
In tough tender strophes.

October 30, 2001

All around the table
Words before bedtime—
Psalms from King James and some of the Wyatt translations;
A *Greensward*, author I cannot remember;
And tortoises, all those poems
By Lawrence, the best wisdom
Re sorrows and abasements, women and men.

WHERE IS THE REST, THE DEAREST PORTION OF MY FAMILY?
Safe at home.

> *In the morning, water*
> *Dowsed a white spider*
> *Out of my razor*
> *When I'd done.*

(My son, I hear, has covered the house in fake spiderwebs.)

Over the phone, the word is
Stay at home tomorrow, Halloween.
Anonymous tips from somewhere in Brooklyn,
Anthrax and explosions.

"There are no just wars."
Happy birthday, Ezra Pound.
Happy birthday, Claudia Keelan.

God help John Keats tomorrow.

November 3, 2001

Cake and icing on her lips
After dancing a little
Because of the new trees
(Palo verde and acacia)
And our roses thriving into November,
Claudia kisses me.

Flowers never spoil. *(They are doors to Heaven op. cit. D.H.*
    Lawrence "Bavarian Gentians"
Singers never age. *(They are doors to Heaven c.f. Walt Whitman*
    somewhere
On the television screen
Cross-legged before a wacky harmonium
One from England sings
To weeping firemen.

So, sometimes, flowers never spoil
Even in the long days after
Lightning strikes the well.

(I am far away writing this—
Tell me, is there water?
How are the trees?

<u>November 30, 2001</u>

At winter night in Salt Lake City

In a bright window   In the dripping bus shelter
Alone in tender display   A schoolgirl smiles far away
A stylist teases her own hair   Into her paperback *The Hobbit*

SOMEONE ELSEWHERE I'M THINKING

Comes ridiculous news
Disappeared remains
Of a hermaphroditic moose

Comes really sad news
Death of George Harrison
I remember impossibly elusive
The prettiest girl in our class
Loved him so

By first light
The snow falls heavily
And, I'm thinking,
More difficultly.
Someone elsewhere
Bringing my good shoes to the ceremony
Flies to meet me.
Every blessed thing is elusive.
All's muddled.
This must pass.

These sentiments grow hair, and wings too.
Just look at the drains, look at the clouds.
John Lennon's death turns 21 today, and one hour
From now, in the theatre over there, the curtain
Rises on the blind kids' matinee: *The Nutcracker.*

Comes terrible news: Shahid Ali dead
Who wept at my table for his mother dead
And balanced then every wild animal slain
In the mts of Kashmir on a silken thread.
He died blind. He was good news.

As I left my hotel this morning,
The television was still talking. It said
These: "like a weapon on its wings" and
"Like a housewife knows her eggbeater."

What do you make of *that*? America   (Arcady)
Is a country of many faults without a flaw.
Why make similes? Why be blind? All we need is love.

In the theatre over there,
Beautiful young bodies
Are dancing in total darkness,
And the darkness cannot touch them.

Mornings of the war that is no war but,
As the man said, new reasons for spitefulness.
All's paused. And inside of that another,
A pause between shepherds and kings.
Dead winter, and the sap is rising.
At the raffle in Blue Diamond, we got the palm tree,
And we drove it home in a wagon under white stars.

Began where?
A place in Brooklyn and the spine of a book
On a shelf—*Journey to the End of the Night,* a trip
I would believe myself taking, ending
In a child who'd traveled for me the whole time.
Mornings of the war are sex in a toilet.
Real sunrise rests today in darkest night
Under a palm tree scarcely visible.
It drinks myrrh direct from Heaven.
When it's full, look for a good day.

New Year

I catch the smell of fuel without peril,
And this morning the moon is enormously pale
Over the Spring Mountains. Someone's cooking
Breakfast outside on a big terrace,
And salt-smoke darkens that moon.
At New Year's nothing's transparent.
Disappearance equals increase, and emptiness
Rises or falls according to no pattern

Because there isn't any pattern yet.
Etc. Etc. Bring out the mustangs now,
And memory, and terror. A birth
Yesterday so near, today seems far.
Should old acquaintance be forgot, sing
Another. And Jesus Christ is the next thing.

Granted, Mary Szybist
Sails the Wind Left Behind, Alessandra Lynch
Sea Gate, Jocelyn Emerson
An Ordinary Day, Xue Di
The Captain Lands in Paradise, Sarah Manguso
Ladder Music, Ellen Doré Watson
Self and Simulacra, Liz Waldner
Live Feed, Tom Thompson
The Chime, Cort Day
Utopic, Claudia Keelan
Pity the Bathtub Its Forced Embrace of the Human Form,
    Matthea Harvey
Isthmus, Alice Jones
The Arrival of the Future, B.H. Fairchild
The Kingdom of the Subjunctive, Suzanne Wise
Camera Lyrica, Amy Newman
How I Got Lost So Close to Home, Amy Dryansky
Zero Gravity, Eric Gamalinda
Fire & Flower, Laura Kasischke
The Groundnote, Janet Kaplan
An Ark of Sorts, Celia Gilbert
The Way Out, Lisa Sewell
The Art of the Lathe, B.H. Fairchild
Generation, Sharon Kraus
Journey Fruit, Kinereth Gensler
We Live in Bodies, Ellen Doré Watson
Middle Kingdom, Adrienne Su
Heavy Grace, Robert Cording
Proofreading the Histories, Nora Mitchell
We Have Gone to the Beach, Cynthia Huntington
The Wanderer King, Theodore Deppe
Girl Hurt, E.J. Miller Laino
The Moon Reflected Fire, Doug Anderson
Vox Angelica, Timothy Liu
Call and Response, Forrest Hamer

ALICE JAMES BOOKS has been publishing exclusively poetry since 1973. One of the few presses in the country that is run collectively, the cooperative selects manuscripts for publication through both regional and national annual competitions. New regional authors become active members of the cooperative, participating in the editorial decisions of the press. The press, which historically placed an emphasis on publishing women poets, was named for Alice James, sister of William and Henry, whose fine journal and gift for writing went unrecognized within her lifetime.

TYPESET AND DESIGNED BY MIKE BURTON
PRINTED BY THOMSON-SHORE